A ROOKIE BIOGRAPHY

GEORGE WASHINGTON CARVER

Scientist and Teacher

By Carol Greene

CHILDRENS PRESS®
CHICAGO

This book is for James Mann.

George Washington Carver (ca. 1864-1943)

Library of Congress Cataloging-in-Publication Data

Greene, Carol.
    George Washington Carver, scientist and teacher / by Carol Greene.
        p.   cm. — (Rookie biography)
    Includes index.
    Summary: Describes the life and accomplishments of the former slave
who became a scientist and devoted his career to helping the South
improve its agriculture.
    ISBN 0-516-04250-5
    1. Carver, George Washington, 1864?-1943—Juvenile literature. 2. Afro-
American argiculturists—Biography—Juvenile literature.
3. Agriculturists—United States—Biography—Juvenile literature.
[1. Carver, George Washington, 1864?-1943. 2. Agriculturists. 3. Afro-
Americans—Biography.] I. Title. II. Series: Greene, Carol. Rookie
biography.
S417.C3G75   1992
630'.92—dc20
    [B]   92-7374
                                                       CIP
                                                       AC

George Washington Carver
was a real person.
He was born around 1864.
He died in 1943.
Carver's work with crops
helped many people.
So did his work with people.
This is his story.

TABLE OF CONTENTS

This statue of George Washington Carver as a boy
stands near Diamond Grove, Missouri.

Chapter 1

The Little Plant Doctor

Ⴤ ᴐᴄ Ⴤ ᴐᴄ Ⴤ ᴐᴄ Ⴤ ᴐᴄ Ⴤ ᴐᴄ Ⴤ ᴐᴄ Ⴤ ᴐᴄ Ⴤ ᴐᴄ Ⴤ ᴐᴄ Ⴤ ᴐᴄ Ⴤ ᴐᴄ Ⴤ ᴐᴄ

George knew the story well.

One cold night,
when he was just a baby,
raiders from the south
burst into the cabin.

They grabbed George
and his mother, Mary,
and took them to Arkansas.

A friend found baby George
and brought him back
to the Carver farm
near Diamond Grove, Missouri.
But Mary had disappeared.
George never saw her again.

"Tell me about my mother,"
George would ask later.
Then Susan Carver would cry.
She missed Mary too.

Susan and Moses Carver
had owned Mary as a slave.
But they loved her,
and they loved her sons.
They raised George and his
brother Jim as their own boys.

Moses Carver bought George's mother, Mary, for seven thousand dollars on October 9, 1835. A copy of this bill of sale is shown below.

Recived of Moses Carver Seven Hundred Dollars in full consideration for a Negro girl named Mary age about Thirtien years who I warrant to be sound in body and mind and a Slave for life Given under my hand and Seal this 9th day of October A.D. 1835

Witness Jno. Dade Jr

Wm P. McGinnis (Seal)

George (left) and his older brother, Jim

Jim was strong.
He helped with the farm.
George was often sick.
He helped around the house.

But George liked
the outdoors, too.
Most of all, he liked
to be alone in the woods.
George had his own
secret garden there.

He grew all kinds of plants.
He made sick plants well
and weak plants strong.
People called George
"the plant doctor."

But George wanted
to know much more.

"I wanted to know
the name of every stone
and flower and insect
and bird and beast,"
he said later.

"I wanted to know
where it got its color,
where it got its life.
But there was no one
to tell me."

The Carvers went to church
in Diamond Grove every Sunday.
But George couldn't go
to school there
because he was black.

A scene at the Visitor Center of the George Washington
Carver National Monument in Diamond Grove, Missouri, shows
George and his brother playing marbles.

Susan and Moses Carver
helped him learn to
read and write at home.
But George needed a real school
and real teachers.

So when he was about 12,
he set off on his own
to find a place to learn.

Chapter 2

A Place to Learn

First George went
to a black school
in Neosho, Missouri.
But he knew almost
as much as the teacher.
He couldn't learn there.

So he went to
Fort Scott, Kansas.

Opposite page: Photo of Carver
as a young college student

Many white people there
hated black people.
George saw them
kill a black man
in a horrible way.
That was enough for him.
He left.

For the next few years,
George moved from
one Kansas town to another.
He learned about art,
books, and plants.
He also made good friends.

George Washington Carver and his classmates at Simpson College

George ended up at
Simpson College in Iowa.
People of all colors
were welcome there.
George studied art.
He was good at it.

Carver studied art at Simpson College

But George felt that God
had a special plan for him.
God wanted him to help
other black people.
Art was not
the best way to do that.

So George found
one more place to learn—
Iowa State University
at Ames, Iowa.
He studied plants and farming.

George got two degrees
from Iowa State.
He was in charge of
the university's greenhouse.
He even did some teaching.

George did so well that
other schools wanted him
to work for them.

Carver wore
this uniform
at Iowa State
University.

Booker T. Washington

Then Booker T. Washington
asked him to come
to Tuskegee Institute
in Tuskegee, Alabama.
And George knew that
was the place for him.

Chapter 3

"Live at Home"

Tuskegee Institute was a poor school with poor land and poor farmers all around it.

George Washington Carver got busy right away, starting with the land.

Carver's Iowa State
University graduation picture

George Washington Carver (front row, center) photographed
with the other teachers at Tuskegee Institute

He saw that too many
farmers planted cotton.
Farmhouses looked like islands
in a sea of cotton.

But cotton took good things
out of the soil
and put nothing back.
You couldn't eat it either.

George Washington Carver working in his lab

Carver studied other crops.
Cowpeas grew well
and put good things
into the soil.
Sweet potatoes also did well.
Farmers could eat those crops.

Soon farmers were coming
to Tuskegee to learn from Carver.
He visited them, too.

"Live at home,"
he told them.
"Don't buy your food
from the store."

He wanted the farmers to grow
fruits and vegetables.
He said they should raise chickens
and eat their own eggs.
He even gave recipes
to the farmers' wives.

Carver also showed farmers
how to make compost—
a food for the soil
made from dead plants.

Carver knew that farmers must care about the health of the soil.

He showed them how to
make their soil healthy.
He told farmers to dig
old plants into the soil.
That would help it too.

Carver had many jobs
at Tuskegee.
He taught students,
ran the farm, and
went to many meetings.
Sometimes he got tired.

But each day,
before the sun rose,
he walked in
the woods.

"When other folk
are still asleep," he said,
"I hear God best
and learn His plan."

Helping poor farmers
was a big part
of that plan.

Chapter 4

"Plant Peanuts!"

The boll weevil was
a busy little insect.
It gobbled up cotton
and wiped out farmers.

"Forget cotton," Carver
told the farmers.
"Plant peanuts!"

Some farmers did, and
the peanuts grew well.
Children loved them.
But what else could
you do with peanuts?

Carver decided to find out.

He went into his lab.
He took peanuts apart.
He put them together again.
He studied those peanuts
inside and out.

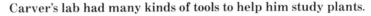

Carver's lab had many kinds of tools to help him study plants.

Carver shows off some of the things he made
from peanuts, including milk and cream!

When he was done,
he had made 300 things
just from peanuts.
He made coffee and soap,
salad oil and ink,
pickles, paper, and milk.

Carver also made
new things from
sweet potatoes,
wood shavings, clay,
and old plant stems.

He saw that *nothing*
should be wasted.
Everything had a job.
You just had to
figure out what
that job was.

Carver didn't sell
the things he made.
That wasn't his job.
But he showed them
and talked about them.

In 1942, automobile manufacturer Henry Ford gave Carver a new, modern lab for his work with plants. Guests at the ceremony ate sandwiches and salads made by Dr. Carver from weeds and wild vegetables.

He even talked to
a committee of
the United States Congress.
He told them about
peanuts and sweet potatoes.

The committee said
Carver could talk
for just ten minutes.
But once he started,
they wouldn't let
him stop.

Carver talked to the committee
for almost two hours,
and when he was done,
they all stood up
and clapped for him.

Chapter 5

A Famous Man

As time went by,
big companies asked
Carver to work for them.
They would pay him
a lot of money.

Carver received thousands of letters from
people who had heard about his work.

George Washington Carver (right) with his assistant, Austin W. Curtis, Jr.

But Carver always said no.
He still believed in
God's plan for him.
He was a teacher, and
he would stay a teacher.

Students at Tuskegee
could visit Carver
whenever they wanted.
He listened to them,
helped with their problems,
and even gave them money.

Many people had been
mean to Carver
because he was black.
He wanted to change
that meanness in people.

A band concert at Tuskegee Institute. Inset: A class at Tuskegee

So he worked with young
people—black and white.
He called them
his boys and girls.
Carver didn't have a wife
or children of his own.

Carver also talked
at colleges, but not
about black and white.
He talked about nature
and all its wonders.
He showed all the new things
he'd made from plants.

Carver grew plants in a greenhouse so that he could study them.

Carver stirs a new product he made from peanuts.

George Washington Carver was a great scientist,
but he never lost his love for art.

People looked and listened.
Then, all at once,
some of them understood.
The color of someone's skin
did not mean a thing!

All through his life,
Carver had saved money.
He lived at Tuskegee.
He wore old clothes.

Now he used that money
to start a foundation
so that his work could go on
after he died.

He started a museum, too.
It held his collections
and many of the things
he made in his lab.

George Washington Carver
was a famous man now.
He won many awards
for his work.

The U.S. postmaster general hands
Carver the first sheet of stamps
printed to honor Booker T. Washington.
Later, a stamp was issued to honor
Dr. George Washington Carver (inset).

Carver met President Franklin D. Roosevelt at
Tuskegee Institute (above). This bronze bust of Carver (below)
at Tuskegee honored Carver's "40 years of creative research."

Carver and two other men received the Roosevelt Medal
for their work. Left to right: Major General Frank
R. McCoy (national defense); Dr. George Washington Carver
(science); Carl Sandburg (literature); James R. Garfield,
(president of the Roosevelt Memorial Association)

But what he liked best
was that eighteen schools
were named for him.

Carver died on
January 5, 1943.
He was almost eighty.

Carver continued working and learning all his life. At the Carver National Monument (above) near Diamond Grove, Missouri, visitors can learn more about the many accomplishments of this amazing man.

He was buried at
Tuskegee Institute, the
place where he helped
so many others learn.

Important Dates

1864   Spring—Born near Diamond Grove,
Missouri, to Mary and an unknown father

1877   Left home for Neosho, Missouri

1890   Went to Simpson College, Indianola, Iowa

1891   Went to Iowa State University, Ames, Iowa

1896   Began teaching at Tuskegee Institute,
Tuskegee, Alabama

1916   British scientists made him Fellow of the
Royal Society of Arts

1921   Spoke before committee of United States
Congress

1923   Given Spingarn Medal by National
Association for the Advancement of Colored
People

1939   Began the George Washington Carver
Museum
Given Roosevelt Medal

1940 Began the George Washington Carver
     Foundation

1943 January 5—Died at Tuskegee, Alabama

1951 George Washington Carver National
     Monument established on the Missouri farm
     where he was born

INDEX

Page numbers in boldface type indicate illustrations.

PHOTO CREDITS

ABOUT THE AUTHOR

Carol Greene has degrees in English literature and musicology. She has worked in international exchange programs, as an editor, and as a teacher of writing. She now lives in Webster Groves, Missouri, and writes full-time. She has published more than 100 books, including those in the Rookie Biographies series.